Affiliate Marketing

Amazing Guide for Beginners Get First Profit Right Away

© Copyright 2018 by Noah Gladwyn -All rights reserved.

Author reserve all rights to this document. No one is allowed to print, reproduce, copy or mimic any of the passage of this document without written permission of the author. Reviewers are allowed to quote a few lines in the reviews.

Disclaimer

No section, line or paragraph of the publication must be reproduced and transmitted by mechanical, electronic or handwriting mean, such as photocopy, recording or any other system without permission in writing from author and publisher.

The purpose of this document is to share verified information, but the author and publisher will not assume any liability for errors, omission and opposing interoperations of the content herein.

The purpose of this book is entertainment and the views and ideas in the book only belong to the author. These ideas should not be taken as expert advice and commands. The readers are only responsible for their actions for doing anything wrong after reading this book.

Only purchaser and reader are responsible to adhere to the application of laws and regulations in their state for advertising, professional licensing and business practices.

Neither author nor the publisher will assume responsibility or liability for actions of purchaser or reader. All brands and trademarks in this book are for clarification purposes and owned by the owners only. They are not affiliated with the document.

Table of Content

Introduction 5
Chapter 1: What affiliate marketing is 6
Chapter 2: Choosing best niches for affiliate marketing 19
Chapter 3: What benefits that affiliate marketing brings 33
Chapter 4: Mistakes that new affiliate marketers often make 38
Chapter 5: How to build your own affiliate marketing business 43
Conclusion 53

Introduction

The word affiliate marketing is heard and seen a lot on the internet. This book will introduce you to the world of affiliate marketing. Many people make the good career out of it. This is the interesting world. Now let's dive in with me.

Chapter 1: What affiliate marketing is

Affiliate marketing can be explained in this way that people do the work to promote the business's products or services to the other audiences or customers. Other audiences or customers here are the people that did not already know about the business's products or services.

The affiliate marketers help the business reach to these potential customers. The business is the reward the affiliate marketer by some sort of commission or money. The affiliate marketers will have their own strategy to promote the business's products or services.

If you surf online, you will see this strategy which is one of the common thing that bloggers do. When you go to the sites of your favorite bloggers, you will often see the link to the website that have some products or services. These products or services are often related to the information that you are looking.

If you purchase the products or services when you go to that website by clicking on the link, the affiliate marketers or this case is the bloggers will earn the commission. Rewarding or commission depends on the business decide. Some businesses have in percent of sale, and some will give the fixed amount after each of their sale.

The business people or the advertisers will take care of the way they have the link to put on the sites of the bloggers or affiliate marketers. The link will have code on that so the business people know that the customers come from which sites. They will have the clear information about the conversion. They also often track it with the cookies. The link and the special code are the two popular tracking conversion to pay the affiliate marketer.

I will give you the example here to simplify. The company A releases the program V. The company give the chances for people who want to promote its program V that priced at $400. The commission is 50%. The affiliate marketers will earn $200 for each program sale. The more they sale, the more commission earned by the affiliate marketers who promote the program using the special link or special code.

The conversion is important. The business only pay when the customers visit the link and actually purchase the products. The business's products or services will get exposed to many customers. The business will have to pay to commission to the affiliate marketers. However, the business will increase a lot in sale and the big chances to exposed to a lot more potential customers. This is the win win situation for business and affiliate marketers.

The affiliate marketers always choose the products or services that they promote are appropriate, fit with their niches and giving them a nice income. The affiliate marketers often have their own business in the niche also. They want to make sure that they will have to pay the big advertise cost more than their commission to promote with a loss.

Blog is one of the most popular outlet for affiliate marketing. Many people search online everyday for information. They will go to the blog. Blog is the awesome bridge to build the relationship between blogger and readers. The bloggers will reach more and more readers with their quality content.

If the bloggers have recommendations to offers, the readers will usually give a best shot to take a look on that. The bridge is established with trust and value of the content. However, the products and services have to be selected carefully to put on the blog.

The products should related to bloggers' niches and add value for readers. Bloggers cannot just put the random products or services to promote because it may destroy the trust of readers. The trust bridge takes long time to build.

One thing I need to mentioned here that not all of the blogs are good for affiliate marketing. Some blogs have the niches with no real available products or services to promote. Bloggers need to aware when picking the products or services to promote.

Affiliate marketing is interesting

Affiliate marketing is a good career for many people. However, you cannot just treat that like a fun hobby that you can do it very minimum thing and expect get a ultimate money printing machine. Many people fail because of that wrong mindset.

Affiliate marketing has many interesting factors to focus. I will list just couple of things here such as the obvious thing is traffic. I do not need to explain here how important of the traffic. The more people are, the more chances that they check out your promotions.

Next, you need to focus on get the related products or services that you and your business are working on. You cannot pick the random products or services. The quality of the products or services must be good and value to your followers.

The next one is building and improving the bridge of trust between you and your followers. You promote the products or services to the right followers that will buy them. This means right focusing group. Your pitch or your writing content or any form of content deliver to the followers or focusing group have to be clear and value providing.

These are just the basic things to focusing of many things in affiliate marketing. These will help you keep the good reputation between you and your focusing group of potential customers and the bridge of trust will be build stronger and stronger by time. Opposite of these basic things will bring your business unwanted results that nobody wishes to happen.

General ideas of how affiliate marketing and money work

Affiliate marketing is almost happening online. The affiliate marketers have to have the online presence. They also need to have the audience that follow them. Blog is popular, but online presence also has many power tools such as email lists, websites, social media etc.

The affiliate marketer also is the partner of the company that sell the products or services. The partner is affiliated with the company. The affiliate marketers have many other names. Beside named partner, they have names such as associates and internet marketers. These names are all representing for people who do affiliate marketing.

You can promote the products or services to your followers in many ways. Affiliate marketer often write articles or posts to describe the products or services. They also post ad in their sites so the followers can easily see and click in.

Affiliate marketer may have the pages or tools to collect the emails of their followers. They will send out email to talk about the products or services that they want to promote to their audience. Affiliate marketers who influence on social media will also talk, share their thoughts and recommend the products or services to their followers. A lot of useful ways is working for affiliate marketers.

The different special links are provided for each affiliate marketers. The audience or the followers click on the link and make a purchasing transaction. Affiliate marketer will earn their money or commission.

The company will be the one to make sure the purchasing transaction go through. The company will often pay their affiliate in the determined period of time. The other way is certain amount of accumulating money meet the minimum requirement of paying out from the company.

Affiliate marketers in general

Affiliate marketers are affiliated with the company. Beside that, you are the affiliate marketers that are also the owner of you websites or your own business. If the affiliate link is on your website or in your articles, you should always tell and state it clear with your audiences or your followers.

Affiliate marketers should do diligent research to find the best products or services to affiliate with. You should always look carefully about the full functions of the products or services. You should use your best to point out the disadvantages or limits of those products or services.

The products or services that the affiliate marketers use will give them the best experience to judge before promote to their followers. Affiliate marketers just need to apply and then become associated with the company one time. They do not need to apply anytime with single company's product or service. After one time applying to join, they can promote many products or services of the company.

The good products or services is important to promote to your followers or audiences. This next thing is also important. Affiliate marketers should pick the appropriate products or services strongly related to their niches to promote to the audiences.

For example, you build your websites or your business around real estate niche. You have many articles around your niche. You cannot put the affiliate link about fitness products. If you promote the fitness products, your audiences will question your professional heavily.

Your audiences will think you don't know what you do exactly. You may lose may audience or subscribers who follow the content that you provide them to your niche. They may see you as spammer.

That will really harm your affiliate marketer's reputation in the big way because your audience will think you just want to go for quick money not value building by time. The affiliate marketers should always remember to pick appropriate and value added products or services to promote to the audiences. That will pay off for the affiliate marketers many big time in the long period of time.

As affiliate marketers, you have the total right to pick and choose which companies or networks that give you the appropriate and best value products or services. You don't have to stick with just only one if you don't really like to work with that network or that company.

You can also have the total right to pick the networks or companies that give you the highest commission. You do not have to work with only one network. You can work with many network at the same time. This way is really smart because you can see which one is better for you in certain way.

Each company or each network will always have unique terms of service. You should make sure go through them carefully. It will help you avoid of unwanted violations that will effect your level of commission.

Besides the companies or networks, affiliate marketers should also focus on the internal such as their article content about the products, the banners, size and font of the letters, the images, the structure of the websites and so on. These things will help the audiences is easily interesting and click to explore the affiliate links. These will result the higher commission level for the affiliate marketers.

Products or services of affiliate marketing

You need a deep look to select what products or services to promote to your audiences through your online presence. You will notice that you use and really like a lot of products or services in your niches without even recognize it.

You already have experience with these products or services, and in these cases there are the big chances that these products or services are really awesome opportunities to promote to your followers. Affiliate marketers can use couple general tips to easy narrow their products or services to promote.

First is the products or services that the affiliate marketers have experience using and really like within their niche. You just need to go search on the website of that company and look for the link said affiliate or referral or similar word choice like that. You can apply and become their associate to promote those products or services.

Next, you can always try Google to find the affiliate program to promote. You should put the keywords or the phrase in the search box. You will put what the product you want and with the phrase affiliate program or affiliates behind and press search. You should patient and try couple time refresh the search keywords. You can also go on pages after pages because sometimes the products or services that you want to promote may not in the first page of Google search.

Another way is taking a look at the people who are on the same niche of your business. I am sure that they will have some sort of online presence such as blogs, websites. You can go to their websites or blogs to see what are the products or services that they promote.

You then evaluate those products or services to make sure that they are really good for your niche and you have the right to promote them. You will learn and see a lot of products or services that you did not think of, and they are really available in your niche.

In the affiliate marketing world, it has the affiliate networks or affiliate companies. If you become affiliate marketer with these networks or companies. They may have products or services for you to promote within your niche.

These networks or companies is acting like a middle man for affiliate marketing. Many companies or organizations will give their affiliate programs for these networks to help them spread more to different affiliate marketers in different niches quicker. It will save companies or organizations a lot of value time to focus on other important things.

Affiliate network of affiliate marketing

In the affiliate marketing world, Affiliate networks or affiliate companies are often in the middle of the marketing business. They are middle man. Like I mentioned above, they receive the affiliate programs which is products or services from companies or organizations. This is one end.

The other end is including affiliate marketers, associates that apply and get accepted to do business with affiliate networks. To be specific, they are business owners with the online presence, bloggers, the people who own websites for their business and so on.

The companies or organizations that want to advertise for their products or services to affiliate network will deal with the affiliate network in terms. The affiliate network will then post the offers for its affiliate marketers or associates know.

Affiliate marketers or associates will see the and work on that offer. They can pick which offers are good and work well for their niche. Many of this offer will be available. In addition, special offers from companies or organizations may require the special application. However, these number of offers are not a lot.

Affiliate marketers will be really selective about the products or services in this step. Affiliate marketers should understand fully the terms of the products or service that they choose to promote.

You will have a comprehensive look about the appearance of the product such as banners, images and many other details. After you give the final decision to choose the products. The code of the special link will be provided. The link is the one that you use for promotion this product to your audiences.

Affiliate network really has an important role in marketing world. Affiliate network is created to fit the needs in the affiliate marketing business. Many companies and affiliate marketers prefer to do the business or transactions with affiliate network.

Affiliate network helps the companies or organizations save time and energy by advertise their products or services to the bigger scale of potential customers. Companies or organizations can set the terms and clear business details with affiliate network easily.

Besides that, Affiliate network helps the affiliate marketers to find the appropriate and good products or services in just only one place. A lot of steps will be eliminate for the affiliate marketers. You can focus on promote the products with your strategies. You can also more focus on your own niche business to scale it up faster.

Affiliate network is the important middle man. It also has its good and fair share of profit. It helps the affiliate marketing world run smoother in many aspects. Affiliate network has its own terms and conditions when it deals with companies and affiliate marketers.

Chapter 2: Choosing best niches for affiliate marketing

Affiliate marketing is an interesting business. Potential affiliate marketers will want to start right away. First, they will have to decide the direction for their business. That means choosing the best niches.

Choosing the right niche will take quite amount of time at first, but it will pay off big time. Your affiliate marketing business will run smoother and scale up faster in the right direction. This is an important starting point.

The niche is

Niche is a section in the whole big market. You will just focus on that section that you choose. You will provide your target followers or audiences with specific products or services. The niche is often narrowing down to specific things, and it cannot be too broad or too general.

You have pick your niche first before your methods or strategies are applied in your affiliate marketing business. For example, it will make things way more easy if you pick your own niche before creating your own business website.

Then you will have a clearly plan to know what you will put in the website. Your website should just address your specific niche. You cannot put unrelated products or services to your audiences. The audiences will establish the healthy relationship with you through products or services that you have in your niche.

Where to start to have ideas for niche

As affiliate marketers, you choose the niche that you like and the market like too. You can choose the niche related to your passion and hobby. You can choose the niche that provide value for your market or you audience. This niche is not your passion niche, but it is what the market needs.

The niche have to suit you and the market. When you are brainstorming the ideas, those ideas are often the niche ideas. Business transactions happen everyday in the world with billion of people involve.

You can see the big advantages of affiliate marketing right here. That is the internet. Affiliate marketers can reach billion of people around the world by their online presence. People nowadays use internet in many aspects of their life not just only business transactions.

You can earn quite good amount of money if you pick a fit niche. It is not completely required. However, if you select the niche that fit with your passion and the market needs or wanted, that will be a perfect combination.

People have tendency that they do good on what they love. When that is your fascinating niche, you will work and have desire to be successful more. You will enjoy to work. Even you have to go extra miles and time, you will be happy that you did it. The final results are that your productivity will be high and way more than your expectation in the beginning.

You first are brainstorming the niche ideas, then you will pick the best niche which you think that fit you. You will have to set up your online presence with that niche. The best way is starting to provide value content and at the same time increase your followers or audiences.

Next, you can establish the good interactions or relationships with the people who are also in that niche and have experience. This step is really good. You will learn a lot of value lessons from them. You will avoid many newbie mistakes.

You receive value information with the people are in your niche. At the same time, you should be willing to help other people as well. This will help you gain the good online presence in the community of that niche. Receiving and offering have to be always in balance.

This next one is also important key that I mentioned above. You have to select the appropriate and valuable products or services in your niche to promote to your audiences. Your audiences will trust you with your value content that you provide over the period of time.

Even though your niche is related to your passion, it will not completely run smoothly. It will have some bumps along the way just like any new start up business. You will need to find the way to solve the problems and make your business better. You should always remember that you have full decision to pick and choose the niche that you are interested.

Niche and specification

Many people are interesting in the different things. Some people will interest in the same thing. We will see them at the group. That is the fundamental of the niche. As affiliate marketers, you will focus to provide the value for that group of people.

It means that you focus on your niche. Is it that more easy for your job? You just need to take a good look at what people in that group want. Your thinking for the work will align with what you need to do step by step without confusions.

Your niche should always be narrowing down to specific area or market. You will be easy to communicate and keep in touch with your followers or your audiences. As common sense, you will think that if the niche is big and wide, you will have more followers and make more money.

It is not completely true that the big niche is good. With the broad niche, you will have the hard time to communicate or provide exactly content or products that your audiences want or need.

Moreover, that will be double hard for the new affiliate marketers. The new marketers will have to compete in the larger scale with more experienced marketers and encounter with many unwanted distractions. This is really the hard battle to win for newbies.

You can see that specification for your niche will give you more advantages. You know exactly what group of people that you want to serve and promote products or services. These products or services will be more relevant to what your audiences need or want. The good result is that your audiences will more likely check the products out and buy them.

The affiliate marketers sometimes unintentional pick the broad niche or not specific enough. It happens with any marketer at least one in the business. I give you an example right here. The affiliate marketer pick the outdoor activities niche.

With the first quick look, you can see this is a good niche about outdoor activities. However, this is really a broad niche and completely not specific at all. In outdoor activities, you can have many specific niches such as fishing, hiking, soccer, kayaking and so much more. You will get completely distractions without clear direction on what to focus and what is your real audiences.

Affiliate marketing is also a business. You will make mistakes a long the way, but that is a important part to growing you business. You should not discourage when you pick the not good fit niche. Even you pick too broad niches couple times, it is still fine. You know that you won't give up, and you always will have trial and error in your business.

Niche and its own importance

In this affiliate marketing world, you have million of niches to pick. In each niche, you will see that it has many of the sub-niches. One of the best way you can do is that focus on the small niche. Small and specific niche is the key.

You start with small and specific niche, and your content will fill up quicker with the demand of the followers. You will build the bridge of trust faster with your own audiences. Oppositely, the board niches will take you double, triple or even more time to provide content and build the bridge of trust with your audiences.

Problem and solution niche

People use mostly internet nowadays. They often search the solutions for the problems that they encounter on the internet also. As affiliate marketer, the solution niche is always a good option to get in.

Affiliate marketers have to do the research to see what are the problems. Then you have to see how demand of the market. You must find the good solutions to provide for your audiences or your followers.

With solution niches, you can easy to find what are your target audiences. You can also easy to promote the products or services that solve those problems because the market or target audiences really need the solutions for specific reason.

I give you some of the obvious problem and solution niches such as the housewife wants to earn extra income by work from home, the people want to follow certain healthy diet to improve their health, the people want to learn to earn become financial freedom and so much more.

You can see here that you provide the solutions that promote products and services for the really need of the market. You don't have to guess or hope that your products or services will work. Your valuable content will match with the market needs immediately.

With the problem and solution niche, you should always determine your target audiences that are really in the need for effective solution. Then you see and categorize what is the level of buying from your followers.

Next your online presence is important because this is how you communicate and build the trust with your followers. Then you can promote the services or products to your followers to earn commission.

When you first start on affiliate marketing, you should not get in the niches that are unknown. You will get distractions and failure easily. You should focus on the niches that are established to be profitable. You use your online presence, tools and content to focusing highly on those profitable niches.

You should do the diligent research and keep update new information about your market or target audiences. That will help a lot in your business because you and your target audiences will always be on the same page. Your strategies or campaigns will attract more your target audiences.

Niche and valuable content

You always have to provide relevant content about your niche on your online present such as blogs or websites. This is an effective way for you to reach to more target audiences. You have to provide content regularly. The more regular content is the better.

You should avoid the attitude that you will provide the content whenever you like or want it. You have to treat this like the real important task in your affiliate marketing career. You can create the content by yourself. You do the research on your own and selecting the best and relevant information for your content.

However, if you have extra capital for your business, you can outsource to the professional that create the content for you. You should give them the clear instructions and the outline in detail what do you really want in your content.

Moreover, you can join the trustworthy forums or communities in your own niche to see what other people discuss about such as new trends, up to date news, new emerging problems or ways to do things faster and more effective.

When you see the new emerging problem, you should provide the good content about that. At the same time, you should affiliate to promote the products or services that solve that problem. You will earn the commission really quick. This habit will help you always on top of things in your own affiliate marketing business.

Niche and affiliate links

In your blogs or websites, you will provide relevant content, but you should never forget to include the affiliate links. You do not need to have just only one affiliate link of one product or one service.

You can have multiple affiliate links of different products or services that are still related to your own niche. The most products that you see are information videos, online video courses, software, formulas, ebooks, etc.

When you are new to the niche, you should start with just one product or service. It will help you build strong trust with your audiences. You will increase provide value content.

The more content that you have on your online presence, you can promote more variety products or services of your niche over period of time. You will have the strong foundations in your online business.

For example, your niche is doing yoga. You can promote at first the good ebook about yoga and how yoga it is very good for the health. Then when you add more relevant content, you can add more products or services such as the video series about doing yoga properly, yoga equipment, yoga clothes, etc.

Besides providing relevant content in your niche, you can also create your online presence by review the top products or services in your niche. First you have to do the research to find out what are the best products or services in the niche.

Next you should check that these products or services will or will not accept the affiliates and other requirements. If they have affiliate programs, you should write the detail review on each product or services with the affiliate link in the same article.

Potential customers will look for the products or services that they want to purchase to solve the problems. The reviews help the potential customers know more about the products or services. They also help customers deciding to buy the products quicker. That will help a lot for your business.

You can create a blog or website just for the purpose of review the top products or services in that niche earn good commission. This review strategy is very effective in the long run, and you also have to keep update new information for your products review sites.

Niche and blog in affiliate marketing

The most important thing in affiliate marketing is affiliate link. If the potential customers click on the affiliate link and purchase the products or services, you will earn your commission. The blog or the website is just one of the tool to help put the affiliate link on.

This means that some affiliate marketers have a different method or way to deliver their affiliate links to the potential customers. The method is paid ads. Paid ads is a strong method, and you will also reach a lot of potential customers to promote your products or services in your niche.

In affiliate marketing world, it will be a mistake if you just depends on just one method to reach the potential audiences. As a newbie, you should not use paid ads right away because you may get a loss if you do not plan your campaigns effectively.

You should get your feet wet in the water first by creating a blog or a website to understand the basic of affiliate marketing. You will have more touch how to set up the website, and how to put and move around the affiliate links in your relevant content to promote the products.

With the blog or website, you will need to provide the valuable content. This way is more about organic traffic comparing to paid ads. You build the reputation and trust with your audiences over the period of time. You will then know which the relevant products or services are to promote to your audiences.

Paid ads cost quiet amount of money. Creating a blog or a website is not totally. It costs money too. However, the amount is way lesser because you will mostly build the organic traffic. You will need a domain name and a web hosting.

The total cost is under $80 per year for those services. They also provide supporting service to answer your questions about running your blog or your website. That seems like a great deal to start for the newbies.

Overall of choosing niche

As affiliate marketers, it is key to have your online presence such as blog or website to target only one niche. You should never have products or services of multiple niches that appear on the same website. They will distract your business, and they will also confuse and mislead your audiences.

If you focus and develop on one niche, you will get way more sale and earn way more commission. Your target audience or your followers will grow quicker because you know exactly your purpose. It will also eliminate ton of distractions in your business.

On your website, you provide the valuable content for your target audiences. Nothing is better than providing the relevant solutions for your target audiences. The more solutions you have for different problems in your niche are the better.

Your followers will form the trust level quickly with your business. Trust between you and your followers is always the important key in affiliate marketing. At the same time, you will promote the relevant products or services through the affiliate links.

As the new affiliate marketers, you will need time to build up your reputation and trust level within your niche and your target audiences. It depends on people that some may take longer time or shorter time than others.

Therefore, you want to dedicate valuable content for your niche as much as you can and as fast as you can. You want soon to become the experienced affiliate marketers in your niche. At that time, the trust level is so firm and high. Almost of relevant products or services that you promote to is checked out or bought by your target audiences.

In your niche, you can also choose high quality products or services to promote. These products or services will give you higher and better commission. They are really worth of your research time.

As you see, the price may be a little bit higher, but the quality will help you win your audiences over, especially the products or services can solve the problems effectively. At the same, you should not just target on the niche have high commission products or services. You should get in the niche that you think you will be a real expert in the future. It will always be a big plus if you have a passion for that niche.

Chapter 3: What benefits that affiliate marketing brings

Affiliate marketing is always an interesting topic. It is a good opportunity for affiliate marketers that want to make extra money or full time income. Besides that, affiliate marketing is also giving a lot of benefits for its affiliate marketers and the whole business world in general.

The cost is often fixed

Affiliate marketing often has a fixed cost. As affiliate marketers, you will know exactly the cost that you spend on your marketing expenses. You can stay proactive and have a full control in your business.

This is working both sides because the company that provide the products or services to the affiliate marketers also know exactly its marketing expenses. The company just have to pay when its products or services was sold to the customers that come from the link of affiliate marketer.

Grow the brand faster

Many companies use affiliate marketing because affiliate marketers can help to spread faster the brand name of the company to their target audiences or potential customers. Each affiliate marketer has own audiences or followers in the niche.

This will help the brand name of the company appear to hundred thousand or even millions of target audiences. Moreover, It is a win win situation. Affiliate marketers provide the valuable content, and the content will help the audience engage more and increase the trust level. Affiliate marketer's own brand will grow faster as well.

Ads always get to right audiences

The affiliate marketers have a good knowledge about the followers or audiences. You create the content to build trust level with your audiences on your blogs or websites. This means that you have the clear fundamentals about what your audiences are really looking for.

When you create ad campaigns, they will completely target to the right audiences. You will spend the money on the ad campaigns effectively. Advertising cost is often one of the biggest cost in online business and business in general.

Your ads will be more standout to your target audiences than the general ads. With the online business presence, you will know many networks for paid ads. Nowadays, there are two popular networks are Facebook ads and Google Adwords.

You can reach to million of people with these two networks. However, it still depends on the budget that you want to spend. You have to calculate in detail the cost of the paid ads. Is the paid ads worth for your new business, etc.

Provide the clear financial picture

Affiliate marketing will always give you a clear picture about your cost, your revenue and your gain. You can easily keep track of your accounting. You spend this much on the ad campaigns or running and maintaining your online presence.

You promote these products or services to earn commission. In the earning way, you can also keep track of how much customers that bought the products or services through your affiliate links. You can also know which affiliate links from which companies that your audiences prefer more.

Diversity ways to approach affiliate marketing

You will have diversity ways to get the job done in affiliate marketing. Many tools or forms or services are available for affiliate marketers. You can get a lot of important things done at the same time.

When you integrate those tools or forms in your affiliate marketing business, you will improve your promoting products or services conversion. You can also improve your traffic by providing what your audiences want at right time.

Very easy to market

Marketing the products or services is costing a lot of time and effort. Affiliate marketing helps the products or services reach to the potential customers way more easy. Affiliate marketers are already professional in their niche. It will save ton of time and effort for the companies and the affiliate marketers. Some experienced marketers use the automated process that will save even more time and energy to marketing.

The risk is low

In business, the risk is always considered in the equation. Affiliate marketing is a good business to get in because it is really low risk. You provide the valuable content and put your affiliate links. The potential customers will make the final decisions to click in and purchase or not at all.

The affiliate marketing depends on the niche. However, ever niche will have its own market or target audiences. You will get the traffic in your niche. Some visitors will click in the affiliate links and not buy the products or services. However, a lot of visitors will buy them. You get so much of traffic and also so much of different ways to get traffic.

As affiliate marketers, you do not have to invest a lot of money in your business. You just have to pick the right niche and make sure provide the relevant content in your online presence to reach to your potential audiences. It will take time, but the return will be completely worth it.

Do not have to create your own products

As affiliate marketers, you have all of the rights to creating your own products or services. However, the advantage is that you do not to create your own products. You make money by promoting other companies' products or services.

If you have your own products, you can also promote them with other companies' products to add more value. They are exactly on the same niche that you base your business on. Creating your own products is literally not required in affiliate marketing.

Flexible in time

You still need to discipline with any business that you work on, and affiliate marketing is not exceptional. However, you can work at the time that you think that works best for you. It is not the same with regular business from 8 to 5.

You will not have the certain hours that you have to close or shut down your business. Your online presence will still be on all the time. Your audiences or followers can access any time they want. You may earn big commission even you are sleeping.

Chapter 4: Mistakes that new affiliate marketers often make

Affiliate marketing is bringing many great benefits for affiliate marketers. However, you still have to set discipline and work properly in this business to achieve your goals. As new affiliate marketers, you need to avoid mistakes to achieve your goals. These are often the mistakes that you may encounter.

Get rick quick career

Affiliate marketing is never one of those get rick quick schemes. Many people provide the false advertisement in this business that you will be rich overnight. They do that false advertisement because they have their own agendas such as selling you their own teaching courses or products.

You should always be aware of these false advertisements because these may make you give up on your dream career. You should always remember that affiliate marketing is a business. It like many other legit businesses that it will take time and effort to achieve success.

Patience is also key. Your patience will help you see the long term goals for your business. Your business will may earn some small amount of money. That happens in may other business too, but you still have to discipline with the business process.

These small amount of money are earned over time. If you combine them together, you will see that you earn a lot of money. You earn these money or commissions because you work and discipline on your business process over the time such as weeks or months before.

The new affiliate marketers can easy to get in this business without too much cost. This is really a good business model for newbies. You can learn from the mistakes as you are growing your business.

However, you never will get rich overnight with affiliate marketing when you are the beginners. You should always set the real expectations when you first start on the business. These real expectations will set you off a lot of disappointments and also give you a lot of courage to win in the long run.

Focus just on selling but not providing value for the audiences

It is very common sense that you have to sell and promote products or services to make money in affiliate marketing. However, you cannot grow more in the business if you just focus on selling and promoting only.

If you want to grow and improve your business to make it better, you need to provide relevant and valuable content for your audiences or followers. You will have to be the one to offer the solutions to helping your target audiences. At the same time, you will see that your earning will increase a lot.

When you help your audiences solve their problems instead of just want to take their money, they will put the trust in your business. The trust level is an important key to success in affiliate marketing.

Your audiences will be loyal and come back to you if you provide them with value instead of just the cold business transactions. That is why your promoting products or services must help the audiences solve their problems.

Earning the trust from your audiences is a must. It will help your business stay and grow in the long run. You should not just see the products or services that sell well and immediately promote them to your audiences.

You should do the diligent research to find out which problems that your audience really concern. Then you go and find the good products or services to promote to help them solve the own problems.

Not believing in your true self

When you are new affiliate marketers, you will lack many skills and techniques to work well in your business. That is completely fine. Many people or gurus have agenda to sell their courses, they will mislead you with a lot of confusing methods.

You should believe in your true self. You need to do the diligent research for your niche or your business. You should trust the process that is best apply to you. You will never rush and should take one step at a time toward your goal.

Confidence is important. If you combine the confidence with the love or passion for what you do, you will be successful in that area. Like I mentioned above, success will not happen over night. You keep yourself confidence in any situations and love what you do are keys.

When I said you should take one step at a time, I mean you should also have your short term goals combine with your long term goal. If you just have the long term goal, you will eventually give up because you will encounter a large amounts of work that wait for you ahead.

Your short term goals help you break the work down to the small pieces. You can easy understand them in small details. For examples, how you can make your blog or website looks more appealing, strategies for keywords to reach more audiences, etc. You will know clearly the steps that you need to take to grow.

Not selecting when promote products or services

You should not have the mindset that you will make the quick bucks in affiliate marketing. When you have that thinking, you will not select the right products or services. You will most likely pick the low quality products or services to promote.

Low quality products or services will not only destroy your affiliate marketing business, but also all of your business. They cost business way too much problems than the small quick bucks that you earn.

If you step on the customers' shoes, you will see how harmful those products or services are. The customers bought the products or services to help them solve the problems, but they are not helping. The customers will not happy.

They will not trust your recommendations any more. They also will review and tell other audiences to stay away form what you try to promote. You will lose a lot of audiences because you are the one who promote these products or services. You should always pick the good quality problem solving products or services for your target audiences even you have to go for extra steps to get them.

Chapter 5: How to build your own affiliate marketing business

After you see the common mistakes that new affiliate marketers may encounter, you will find in this section how to build the legit affiliate marketing business. Like I mentioned above, you cannot get rich with affiliate marketing overnight. It takes a lot of trials, time and efforts to becoming better affiliates.

Must get real with affiliate marketing

You should not have the attitude that let's try affiliate marketing because you heard from the people that you know try it. It is not a good attitude to starting on the affiliate marketing journey. It likes any other business, it takes time and effort.

You will need time to learn the real skills to apply for your business. Some skills will take long time to master. You will have to see that affiliate marketing is a long term career that will earn you good income. In affiliate marketing, you get pay by earning commission. You are the owner of your business.

Focus on your future and present goals

You focus on make decent money or commission in the present time. That is necessary to sustain your business. At the same time, you should focus on build the really healthy relationship with your audiences or followers.

That means increasing the trust level over period of time. You also have to stay proactive to see what the future between you and your followers. How they can stay and connect to your business in the long run. Your customers will still follow you on social media, your email list, etc.

The reputation of your online presence is so important. Your commission is good, but that is not important than the trust level between you and your target audiences. Your audiences will have big impact to growing your affiliate marketing business. You must have online presence such as blogs or websites for your business to go forward.

Important needs of website or blog

The websites or blogs are important for affiliate marketing. You may hear that someone earns money of affiliate marketing without a website or a blog. It can be true. That is just another way.

However, you should have a blog or a website. It helps you have an established online presence to your audiences. That is also your property on the online world. Without websites or blogs, you will need other strategies to reach to your target audiences.

It is really good that you have your blog or website. You have strongly online presence without relying on the third parties. Relying on third parties has its own advantages, but the third parties can decide to close your account if something go wrong.

You need your independent online presence because you want your business is stable and growing. I will give the examples. You had an awesome Facebook or other social media profile with a lot of followers.

Things went wrong one day, and your account got blocked or banned. Your business will never recover from that. This is showing you how important to have your own website or blog to interact with your own audiences.

Get the right niche

You choose the niche that are right for you is so key. The right niche will scale up your business really quickly. Choosing the wrong niche will make it so hard to earn your commission. If the niche is your passion, it will be a plus.

You should screen some important questions before you choose the niche such as the niche needs to have available market or target audiences, what the problems are in this niche, where I can get the relevant solutions, how competitive the niche is.

Having passion for what you choose

You can choose any niche you want. You can still work on the niche that you don't actually like and potential earn a lot of money. However, you will easily give up or not pay much attention. You will see the work like obligation instead of passion everyday.

You should focus on the niche that you have passion about. You may not be professional about that niche yet. However, you can do diligent research to master that niche over period of time. You will do better with what the thing you have passion about.

Pay for hosting for your website

I think you may or may not create the free website or blog on free web hosting before. You create those websites for fun sharing or general purpose. However, for business purpose such as affiliate marketing, you should consider the paid web hosting service.

As affiliate marketer, you will potentially earn high commission. You need to paid to get the reliable web hosting service. Your business is the real deal. In affiliate marketing, you will work mostly online.

You need to invest on the good web hosting. The last thing you want is your website does not run properly. You do not want have any trouble to your online presence. Everything must be secure and ready to interact with potential customers.

Web hosting service that you pick must be reliable and trusty. It has to have a good support system. You should do your own research to understand fully its service. You should make sure the web hosting is available 24/7.

When you do your own research, you will find out many of web hosting services. There are some popular ones such as Bluehost, iPage, HostGator, etc. You should choose the service base on you budget and what you expect in the service.

Web hosting is really worth. You should not worry and concern too much when you purchase the right tool for your business. You do it with your confidence. You can use web hosting service that you think is best. If you do not like that service any more and you choose to pick another web hosting service, the new web hosting will help you move your website to its new platform. The change is very simple and free.

Creating website

Before you get a web hosting service, you should create or build a website. You will need the platform to build your website on. Many online marketers use WordPress because it is a popular platform. You can research online and see quite amount of the tutorial videos on how to create a website using WordPress.

Decide products or services to promote

After you pick the niche, you have to pick the relevant products or services to promote or sell. The products or services cannot be all over the places. They have to related to your niche. You should have good knowledge about them.

It will be a plus point if you use or apply the products or services before, and you actually like them. The content that your followers love is fitting with the products or services. You will have the high percent chance to sell them.

You need to increase your reputation and trust level with your target audiences. The promoting products or services have to satisfy the customers' needs. That is the main purpose for your business.

You can also go the extra miles in your business. You should check with the company that you help promote the products or services how they treat and assist the customers. After the sale, you want to make sure that your target audiences are in good care.

Find affiliate products or services

This is the one the important part to earn money in affiliate marketing. You will do your search and go to sites that offer affiliate products or services. You will need to look hard in this step.

Affiliate network sites are having many affiliate products or services from different merchants or companies. You can apply or sign up to be a member of these affiliate networks.

After becoming a member, you can pick and promote the products or services that fit with your niche. In affiliate marketing world, the affiliate networks are very many. Some affiliate of popular affiliate networks that you may be heard of are Clickbank, JVZoo, ShareASale, etc.

Most of affiliate networks are pay per sale. In addition, affiliate network also has pay per click such as AdSense. There are many different ways to get pay by affiliate networks. You should do your research well.

Besides the affiliate networks, merchants or companies have their own affiliate links or affiliate programs to provide for affiliate marketers. You just need go straight to their websites to become affiliate.

They will have clear information and requirements for you to follow. You should always aware about the reputations of merchants or companies in your niche. Some of them may not have good reputations that pay commission on time for their affiliates. You must select to be affiliate with the good merchants or companies.

You should keep eyes on the competitors or the people who are same niche with you. You will do your research on which products or services that sell well on their sites and avoid which products or services do not.

Put affiliate links and banners in the right place

You should concern to put the banners and links in your relevant content. They will be more effective because the target audiences can see them when they check out your content. The relevant content is what make your audiences decide to check out and make the purchase of the products or services.

Content must relevant and helpful

The content is the key in affiliate marketing. You will get and increase your target audience because of valuable content. You build and increase the trust level with your target audiences. You will see the increase commission in your business.

You always have to provide the best and relevant content for your audiences. You cannot have the so so just good enough content. You have to do the awesome job to get the potential customers buy the products or services after they see your content.

Interact with the audiences

You should also have a landing pages to interact in certain level with your target audiences. You can ask them email addresses and offer them something is value in exchange. You will interact with your audiences in another level.

You can offer them the free report with good information, alert your audiences on email when the new valuable content is ready. Besides, you can share value information on your other social media.

Aim to success with the good plan

You do affiliate marketing to earn money or commission. You should always remember that. You have to have a clear plan to provide valuable content and monetize your target audiences in the right way.

You will be clear with your audiences that you want to help them to solve their problems by promoting the relevant products or services. You have to put your affiliate links or banners in your content because your audiences will expect it and appreciate you for that.

Fit products give good profit

You should constantly pick and hunt the relevant and fit products or services for your content. You will not make any money if you pick the wrong products or services to promote. Your awesome content will become useless.

The content and the products or services must support each other in any aspect. That is when the target audience will make the purchase. You pick a product or service, and you have the feeling that your audience will not fit for your content. You should stop there and go for the different choice.

You will search for the match products or services. You get the match, and you can try them first to see how it work for your niche and your valuable content. You will see the result by first hand experience to decide to pick or drop that product or service.

Conclusion

Thank you for making it through to the end of this book. I am feeling that you enjoy these good contents about what affiliate marketing is, picking the best niche for your affiliate marketing business, benefits of affiliate marketing bring for affiliate marketers, mistakes to avoid in this business for new marketers, and build a stable affiliate marketing business. Again I really hope that the information in this book will be helpful for you.

www.ingramcontent.com/pod-product-compliance
Lightning Source LLC
Chambersburg PA
CBHW030054230526
45471CB00003B/1085